Critical Thinking in Math

Adapted from
Brain-Compatible Mathematics

Diane Ronis

Critical Thinking in Math

Published by SkyLight Professional Development
2626 S. Clearbrook Dr., Arlington Heights, IL 60005
800-348-4474 or 847-290-6600
Fax 847-290-6609
info@skylightedu.com
http://www.skylightedu.com

President: Carol Luitjens
Executive Vice President, Product Development: John Nolan
Executive Editor: Chris Jaeggi
Senior Acquisitions Editor: Jean Ward
Editor: Anne Kaske
Editorial Assistant: Carrie Straka
Book Formatter: Donna Ramirez
Book Designer: Bruce Leckie
Cover Designer and Illustrator: David Stockman
Production Supervisor: Bob Crump

ISBN 1-57517-839-7

UG

Z Y X W V U T S R Q P O N M L K J I H G F E D C B A
09 08 07 06 05 04 03 02   15 14 13 12 11 10 9 8 7 6 5 4 3 2 1

There are
one-story intellects,
  two-story intellects, and
    three-story intellects with skylights.

All fact collectors, who have no aim beyond their facts, are

one-story minds.

Two-story minds
compare, reason, generalize,
using the labors of the fact collectors
as well as their own.

Three-story minds
idealize, imagine, predict—their best illumination
comes from above,

through the skylight.

—Oliver Wendell Holmes

Contents

Introduction

Critical thinking skills are the mental skills and processes involved in the act of learning, such as remembering and understanding *facts, ideas,* and/or *concepts.* In recent years cognitive psychologists have compiled a great deal of new information about thinking and learning, much of it done in conjunction with neurobiologists interested in how the human brain thinks, learns, and remembers.

Thinking processes describe what goes on in the learner's brain during learning—how knowledge is acquired, organized, stored in memory, and used in further learning and problem solving. It is often helpful to classify knowledge as either declarative—knowledge about something—or procedural—knowledge of how to do something. Some theorists suggest that knowledge begins as declarative and becomes procedural as it is used in solving problems.

For development of conceptual mathematics and mathematical problem solving, building thinking skills and processes is essential. The National Council of Teachers of Mathematics stresses the importance of reading, writing, and discussion for the development of students' mathematical thinking:

7

The development of a student's power to use mathematics involves learning the signs, symbols, and terms of mathematics. This is best accomplished in problem situations in which students have an opportunity to read, write, and discuss ideas in which the use of the language of mathematics becomes natural. As students communicate their ideas, they learn to clarify, refine, and consolidate their thinking. (NCTM 1989)

This position (consolidated from the NCTM's previously published standards) has been reiterated in the new Principles and Standards for School Mathematics (2000), and continues to remain key for the success of *all* students (pre-K–12) in our 21st century technologically advanced society.

This booklet will offer ways to promote critical thinking and make students more conscious of their thinking in three contexts:

- cooperative problem solving,
- reflective discussion and writing about mathematical ideas, and
- steps and strategies for problem solving.

Also offered to teachers is a hierarchy of instructional tasks to guide their own choices as they move students to more challenging and rewarding mathematical tasks.

SkyLight Professional Development

Promoting Critical Thinking in Cooperative Groups

> Students' understanding of mathematical ideas can be built throughout school years if they actively engage in tasks and experiences designed to deepen and connect their knowledge. Learning with understanding can be further enhanced by classroom interactions, as students propose mathematical ideas and conjectures, learn to evaluate their own thinking and that of others, and develop mathematical reasoning skills. Classroom discourse and social interaction can be used to promote the recognition of connections among ideas and the reorganization of knowledge . . . Moreover, in such settings, procedural fluency and conceptual understanding can be developed through problem solving, reasoning, and argumentation.
>
> —*Principles and Standards for School Mathematics* (2000, NCTM, p. 21)

For students to understand mathematics conceptually, they need to interact with each other as well as the teacher. Students also need to discuss their own ideas about mathematics. For small group work to be successful, the team members must learn to function as a unit. The teacher needs to lay the groundwork for effective group relationships by promoting the cooperative and collaborative social skills associated with positive group relationships, including the following:

9

- Praise good ideas
- Describe feelings
- Express support for one another
- Listen to each other
- Be positive
- Give encouragement

Once the climate for positive group work is established, the teacher's next step is to make the expectation clear that when solving a problem, all students must be able to explain their thinking, to justify their answers, and to explain why an answer is reasonable. When students defend their solutions to others in small groups, they develop a better understanding of the mathematics involved and become more confident about their own ability to solve difficult problems.

The following three expectations need to be discussed with students for the establishment of an environment conducive to small group problem-solving work:

1. Students are expected to work together on their assigned problem and make sure that each member of the group participates.
2. Students are expected to listen to each other carefully, and to then build on each other's ideas.
3. Each individual team member is expected to be able to explain and justify the team solution.

10

The following cooperative group formats use temporary, informal groups that last from a few minutes to one class period. These group formats give students the opportunity to engage in focused discussion before and after a lesson. The following ideas were derived from the work of Johnson, Johnson, and Holubec (1988).

1. *Target Groups:* Before beginning a video, lesson, or reading assignment, student groups should identify what they already know about the subject and identify questions they may have. After the lesson is completed, the groups can answer the questions listed earlier, discuss new information, and formulate new questions.

2. *Neighbor to Neighbor:* Students ask their neighbor something about the lesson. The questions asked should lead to answers that explain a new concept, summarize the most important points of the discussion, or provide important information that might fit the lesson.

3. *Study-Buddies:* Students compare their homework answers, discuss any problems they haven't answered similarly, go over those problems together, and then list the reasons they changed any of the answers. They then make sure that all their answers match. The teacher then grades only one randomly selected paper from each group, and gives all group members that same grade since all their answers should match.

11

4. *Problem Detectives:* Groups are given a problem to solve. Each student must contribute to part of the solution. Groups can decide who does what, but they must show how each member contributed. For alternative strategy, the group can decide on the solution together, but then each group member must be able to independently explain how the problem was solved.

5. *Drill Pairs:* Student pairs drill each other on the facts they need to know until they are certain both partners retain all of the information. This works for math, spelling, vocabulary, grammar, test review, etc.

Promoting Critical Thinking Through Reflective Writing

If group discussion and individual verbalization occurs *before* beginning problem elaborations or reflections, students' chance of success increases. Discussion, reading, writing, and hearing about mathematical ideas is key for improved performance.

According to the NCTM *Principles and Standards for School Mathematics* document:

> Effective learners recognize the importance of reflecting on their thinking and learning from their mistakes. . . . By having students talk about their informal strategies, teachers can help them become aware of, and build on, their implicit knowledge. —*Principles and Standards for School Mathematics* (2000 NCTM, p. 21)

SkyLight Professional Development

Following are some sample questions teachers can use to help guide students to written reflections that will help them to think critically about a problem.

Teachers should ask students to respond to some or all of these questions in writing.

1. Understanding of the Problem
   - Can you tell me in your own words what this problem is about?
   - Is anything missing, or has any unnecessary information been given?
   - What assumptions are you making about the problem?

2. Planning of the Strategy
   - Can you explain your strategy to me?
   - What have you tried so far?
   - How did you organize your information?
   - Is there a simpler problem related to this one that you could solve first?

3. Executing the Strategy
   - Can you show me how you checked your work?
   - Why did you organize your work in this way?
   - Why did you draw this diagram?
   - How do you know whether what you are doing is correct?

4. Review of the Work
   - Are you sure your answer is correct? How do you know this?
   - Could you have solved this problem differently?
   - What made you decide to use this strategy?
   - If I changed the original problem to read . . ., would you still use this same strategy?

5. Mathematical Communication
   - Can you reword this problem using simpler terms?
   - Can you explain why you are doing this?
   - How would you explain what you are doing to a teammate who is confused?
   - Can you create a problem of your own using this same strategy?

6. Mathematical Connections
   - Have you ever solved a problem similar to this one? In what way is it the same? In what ways is it different? (Show the student a different but similar problem, then ask:) What, if anything, is similar about the mathematics in this problem and the one you just solved?

7. Self-Assessment
   - Is this kind of problem easy or hard for you?
   - What makes this type of problem easy? What makes it difficult?
   - In general, what kinds of problems are especially hard for you? What kinds are easy? Why?

14

In a self-reflection, students often write an account of the work completed. They describe their methods and results, and assess what new information they learned. The teacher can structure the reflection by asking students questions that focus on selected aspects of the activity. Sample questions follow.

- What task did you do for your group?
- How did you keep track of your results?
- How confident do you feel about the work you did? Why?
- What new mathematics did you learn?
- How does this new knowledge relate to knowledge you already have?
- What new questions do you now have after completing this activity?

By incorporating these reflective questions into the routine of teaching mathematics, students begin to incorporate this deeper level of thoughtfulness into their own mathematical analysis and learning.

Promoting Critical Thinking Through Problem-Solving Strategies

The steps and strategies of problem solving should also be taught explicitly to improve critical thinking.

Seven-Step Process

A seven-step process students can use will help them move methodically through a problem that might seem overwhelming if approached without a process.

15

Seven-Step Process for Problem Solving

1. Examine the problem.
2. Determine what information is given and what information is implied, or can be deduced.
3. Break the problem down into smaller units so that it becomes more manageable. (Try to find smaller, simpler shapes within the large, complex one.)
4. Plan a strategy—a step-by-step plan you will use to solve the problem. Write out the strategy so that you can check to see if you have completed all the steps at the end.
5. Write out all the formulas you will need for this problem.
6. Solve the problem.
7. Check the strategy you planned to be sure that you have done all the necessary steps, and labeled all answers correctly.

As students engage in problems it can be helpful to have a variety of methods to use for working through any of the steps in the seven-step process if their thinking falters. Teachers may want to create activities for student practice in all of the following methods.

- Brainstorm.
- Make it simpler.
- Use logical reasoning.
- Work backwards.
- Make a picture or diagram.

16

- Make a chart or a table.
- Make an organized list.
- Use or look for a pattern.
- Guess and check.

Heuristics

Heuristics are methods that aid learning through exploration and experimentation, especially trial and error. An example of a problem-solving heuristic is a strategies wheel (see Figures 1 and 2). Students can make a wheel with a piece of cardboard or a paper plate and an arrow attached with a brad through the center. The different sections of the wheel—drawn in—represent the different choices that can be used individually or in any combination to arrive at the solution goal. An arrow pointing to the solution in use keeps the student focused on the particular methodology being used at that moment.

Giving students a strategy wheel helps them choose from among the different methodologies in their repertoire when trying to assess their best solution path. The first wheel (Figure 1) has fewer choices and is more appropriate for students in earlier grades.

More advanced students can have the choice of a greater number of methodologies since these will be used at more sophisticated levels (Figure 2).

17

Simple Problem-Solving Strategies Wheel

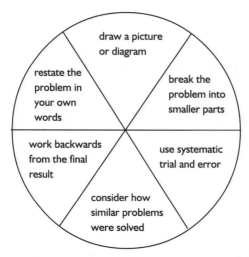

restate the goal in your own words	look for patterns
guess and check	draw a diagram

Figure 1

Advanced Strategies Wheel

draw a picture or diagram

restate the problem in your own words

break the problem into smaller parts

work backwards from the final result

use systematic trial and error

consider how similar problems were solved

Figure 2

SkyLight Professional Development

Reading Problems Carefully and Critically

It is crucial for teachers to explicitly teach students to read carefully and critically. Students must understand and evaluate mathematical problems. Teachers can provide a checklist for reading problems carefully. Before students read a problem, they should read the checklist. As they work through the problem, they should refer to the checklist and make sure they are following the steps.

Checklist for Reading Problems Critically

❑ Read all directions once to get a general idea of the problem or task.

❑ Read the material again to learn the specific directions.

❑ Summarize each direction on paper in your own words.

❑ Pay close attention to the pictures or diagrams provided.

❑ Pause after each direction you read, and make a picture in your mind of what you are supposed to do.

❑ When you come to something important that you don't understand, reread it or ask someone for help.

❑ Use resources such as your textbook glossary or a dictionary to look up any words you don't understand.

❑ Try to think ahead to anticipate any difficulty you might have.

19

Visual and Organizational Strategies

An important strategy aid to thinking is visualization. Visual aids such as graphic organizers, graphic representations, drawings, and diagrams are all examples of organizational strategies.

Graphic organizers provide a visual, holistic representation of facts, concepts, and their relationship within an organized framework. They are effective tools that support thinking and learning by:

- helping students and teachers to represent abstract information in a more concrete format;
- depicting relationships between and among facts and concepts;
- relating new information to prior knowledge; and
- organizing thoughts for writing or problem solving.

Teachers who include graphic organizers as part of their instructional repertoire enhance student learning. Knowledge that has been organized into a holistic conceptual framework is more easily remembered and understood than unstructured, unconnected bits of information.

Graphic organizers can be used prior to instruction as a conceptual framework for the integration of new information. During instruction they help students actively process and reorganize information. Following instruction they help students summarize learning and

20

encourage elaboration, provide students with a structure for review, and help the teacher assess the level of student understanding.

Graphic organizers exist in a variety of forms—as the concept web, flowchart, matrix, concept map, or Venn diagram. The Venn diagram can be used for a number of purposes, such as comparing (see Figure 3).

Graphic representation strategies are learning tools that create symbolic pictures of the structure and relationship of the material. Some examples of graphic representation strategies are networking strategies that require students to depict relationships among concepts or ideas using a diagram format or graph (see Figures 4 and 5), and concept mapping strategies that require students to identify elements of the problem and then note them in proper sequence. Figure 4 can be used with adaptations at any level. Figure 5 can be used with upper- and secondary levels.

The more organized the material is, the more clearly its organization is perceived by the learner, and the greater the learning. Graphic organizers and graphic representations enable visual and spatial learners to "see" what they're thinking. The Math Strategy Graphic Organizer is an example of this kind of visual representation (see Figure 6).

21

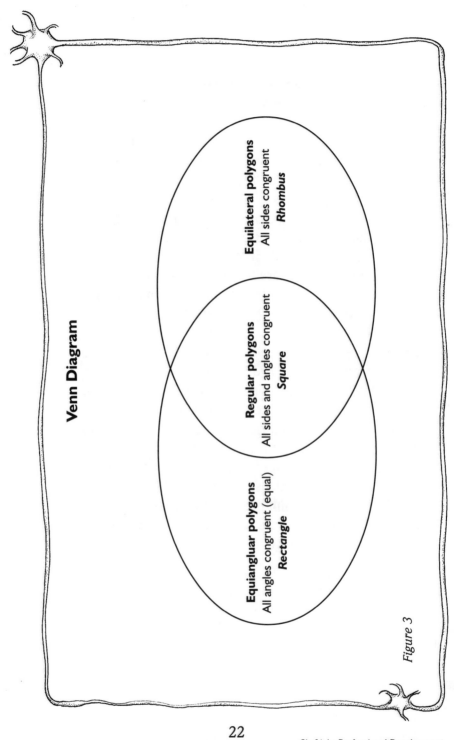

Venn Diagram

Equiangular polygons
All angles congruent (equal)
Rectangle

Regular polygons
All sides and angles congruent
Square

Equilateral polygons
All sides congruent
Rhombus

Figure 3

22

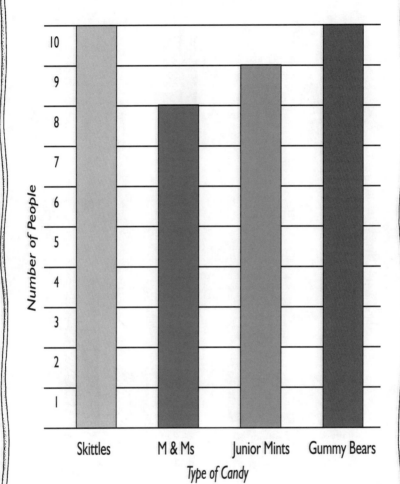

Figure 4

What Do You Cost?

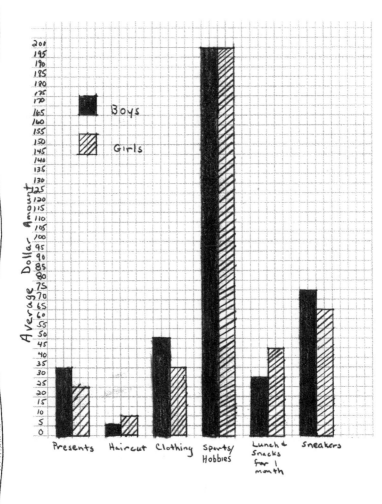

Figure 5

SkyLight Professional Development

Math Strategy Graphic Organizer

Name: _____ Section: _____ Date: _____

1. Restate the question in your own words.

_____
_____
_____
_____

2. List the facts you will need to solve the problem.

- _____
- _____
- _____
- _____

- _____
- _____
- _____
- _____

3. Plan your strategy.

Step A: _____
Step B: _____
Step C: _____

4. Solve the problem:

Step A	Step B	Step C

5. Check: Does your answer make sense?

6. Answer

Figure 6

Patterns

The human brain's innate search for meaning occurs through "patterning." The brain seeks to achieve order from disorder through patterning with schematic maps and categories, both acquired and innate. The brain needs and automatically registers the familiar while simultaneously searching for and responding to novel stimuli. The brain tries to recognize and understand patterns as they occur and to give expression to unique and creative patterns of its own. As students look for patterns, they think about a new problem in relation to others that they have seen before.

As teachers see students' ability to think more critically and approach problems with a stronger repertoire and greater confidence, teachers can use the hierarchy of lessons to allow students to flex their new critical thinking muscles (see Figure 7).

Hierarchy for the Selection and Creation of High-level Mathematical Tasks

Mathematical Tasks—Higher-Level Demand Tasks:
- require sophisticated and complex non-algorithmic thinking;
- require the ability to regulate one's own cognitive processes;
- require students to access relevant knowledge and make appropriate uses of such knowledge in task completion;
- require students to analyze and actively examine any task constraints that might limit possible strategies and solutions; and
- require considerable cognitive effort, and many result in some level of student stress due to the unpredictable nature of the solution process.

Figure 7

SkyLight Professional Development

Procedures with Connections—Higher-Level Demand Tasks:
- focus attention on the use of procedures for deeper levels of understanding;
- suggest general and broad procedures that are closely connected to the underlying concepts rather than narrow procedures and rigid algorithms;
- are presented in different ways, so as to address the multiple intelligences; and
- require some degree of cognitive effort in order to connect with the conceptual ideas that underlie the procedures necessary for comprehension and successful task completion.

Procedures Without Connections—Lower-Level Demand Tasks:
- are algorithmic in that the use of the procedure is either specifically called for or is evident from prior instruction;
- have little ambiguity or complexity, and require limited cognitive effort for successful completion;
- have no connection to the broad underlying concepts; and
- are focused on the production of correct answers rather than mathematical connections, understandings, or explanations.

Memorization—Lower-Level Demand Tasks:
- consist of reproducing previously learned rules, definitions, and formulas or memorizing new rules, definitions, and formulas;
- are not complex or ambiguous, and involve only the replication of familiar material; and
- have no connection to the broad underlying concepts.

(NCTM 2000, National Research Council 2000,
S. Krulik and J. Rudnick 1995)

Figure 7 (continued)

27

Conclusion

Use of the critical thinking frameworks and problem-solving strategies discussed in this booklet will help students learn effective techniques to create order out of what may at first seem chaotic. Such strategies enable learners to set up their own ordered systems for thinking critically and solving problems, and therefore work well with the brain's innate search for order and meaning.

28

Bibliography

Alper, L., D. Findel, S. Fraser, and D. Resek. 1996. Problem-based mathematics not just for the college-bound. *Educational Leadership* 53(8): 18–21.

Caine, R. N., and G. Caine. 1999. *Mindshifts: A brain-compatible process for professional development and the renewal of education,* 2nd ed. Tucson, AZ: Zephyr Press.

Dehane, S. 1997. *The number sense: How the mind creates mathematics.* New York: Oxford University Press.

Fogarty, R., and J. Bellanca. 1986. *Teach them thinking: Mental menus for 24 thinking skills.* Palatine, IL: IRI/SkyLight Training and Publishing, Inc.

Johnson, D., R. Johnson, and E. Holubec. 1994. *The new circles of learning: Cooperation in the classroom and school.* Alexandria, VA: Association for Supervision and Curriculum Development.

Krulik, S., and J. Rudnick. 1995. *The new sourcebook for teaching reasoning and problem solving in the elementary school.* Needham Heights, MA: Allyn and Bacon.

———. 1994. Reflect . . . for better problem solving and reasoning. *Arithmetic Teacher.* February, 41: 334–338.

National Center for Educational Statistics, Office of Educational Research and Improvement. 1996. *Pursuing excellence: A study of curriculum, and achievement in international context.* Washington, DC: US Department of Education.

National Council of Teachers of Mathematics. 2000. *Principles and standards for school mathematics.* Reston, VA: NCTM.

29

National Research Council. 2000. *How people learn: Brain, mind experience, and school.* Washington, DC: National Academy Press.

Ronis, D. 2001. *PBL: Problem-based learning for math and science: Integrating inquiry and the Internet.* Arlington Heights, IL: SkyLight Training and Publishing.

Salmon, M., and C. Zeitz. 1995. Analyzing conversational reasoning. *Informal Logic* 17: 1–223.

Schmidt, W., C. Knight, and S. Raizen. 1997. *A splintered vision: An investigation of U.S. science and mathematics education.* U.S. National Research Center for the Third International Mathematics and Science Study. Dordrecht/Boston, London: Kluwer Academic Publishers.